ARK

KUHL HOUSE POETS

edited by Jorie Graham *and* Mark Levine

ARK

Poems by John Isles

UNIVERSITY OF IOWA PRESS Ψ Iowa City

University of Iowa Press, Iowa City 52242

Copyright © 2003 by John Isles

Printed in the United States of America

Design by Richard Hendel

http://www.uiowa.edu/uiowapress

The publication of this book was generously supported
by the University of Iowa Foundation.

Printed on acid-free paper

Library of Congress Cataloging-in-Publication Data
Isles, John.
    Ark: poems / by John Isles.
       p.   cm.—(Kuhl House poets)
    ISBN 0-87745-860-x (pbk.)
       I. Title.   II. Series.

    PS 3609.S58A88 2003
    811'.6 — dc21   2003040251

03   04   05   06   07   P   5   4   3   2   1

To the memory of my mother and father

CONTENTS

ACKNOWLEDGMENTS

I am grateful to the editors of the following publications in which some of these poems first appeared:
American Literary Review, Black Warrior Review, Boomerang!, Colorado Review, CutBank, Denver Quarterly, Elixir, Fine Madness, First Intensity, Green Mountains Review, Gulf Coast, Phoebe, Pleiades, Poet Lore, Quarter after Eight, Seattle Review, Sonora Review, Xantippe, and *ZYZZYVA.*

This book would not have been possible without the comments and encouragement of many people. I am indebted to my teachers at the Iowa Writers' Workshop, Jorie Graham and Mark Levine for choosing the manuscript, Brenda Hillman, Mary Wang, Sam Witt, D. A. Powell, and Lary Kleeman.

Finally, I am forever grateful to my greatest poetic ally, my wife, Kristen Hanlon.

I

WRONG SEA IS IMPOSSIBLE.

— Odysseas Elytis, "What Convinces" (tr. Olga Broumas)

TO A PRETENDING LEAF

I want to take off your green blouse *because.*
I love the world behind every blouse.

Because underneath skin and heart lie.
I want to say it, *take off your clothes.*

This way you know I feel it the way you do.
Sticky lick at the back of my neck—

locust lick of the September sky—
sweet burden I never asked for.

I feel it when I'm about to pluck you:
The roofers' radio-mariachi loses its accent

inside you—you dance like some body.
Like yesterday's grass, which you are

nothing compared to—like dirt.
Dirt of Indians, one little, two little . . .

I'm waiting for you to fall and kiss
the ground you come from because in that kiss

scatterbrained moths fly backwards,
returning florescence to the flower,

Arcadian dust to the garden arcade.
Because there's a wild man in the jungle.

And a wise man in the desert.
Because in this yard, there's nobody and a leaf,

nobody and your clothes strewn everywhere.

Something is always happening.
Something's getting around to
happening or having just happened,
loitering in the vicinity, drunk in the sun.
It just so happens that nothing is at home.
Our house has everything, garden
with fruit tree, egret pumping across,
white kite with a mind of its own.
Symbol of a harmonious universe,
is what we like to say we say.
The garbage cans hold a symposium
with the moths, and all agree:
The news that sells is no news.
Just blocks from here, a girl
was stabbed to death for ten dollars
and a cell phone and no one
wants to compare this to the natural world.
We awoke to raccoons thrashing
in the rubber wading pool, African
Savannah for its motif: giraffes,
zebras, a rainbow tying it all together.
When we came to this place *forever*
came to mind. Tomatoes, cucumbers,
peppers swell and further convince us.
The grass goes wild, the grass
breaks up the cement path from the door
to the tree with its stewing black fruit.

CARRION DAYS

Yesterday, the woman I never had,
I am constantly having, having been myself, had.
Not only in dream but in the hunger
I follow down the slender fingers of my wife.

*

Whitewashed out as it were, the dead
shape the air with their God-like absence.
Twenty coats makes twenty times removed.
They tenant the white of this room.

*

Where masters outnumber dogs, wilderness
is relative to the leash. Most of the truth
mostly isn't. Redundancies of blue except here,
at ground level, where difference lies.
My father, a keeper of prisoners, loved his prison.
He befriended his German charges.
His souvenirs, a ship-in-a-bottle, a pastoral
painted plate, recall nothing that ever happened.

*

The cows, a patchwork on these wintergreen hills.
The cries, cries of a boy putting a gun
to the head of his playmate. "Blam,"
he says and drags the outlaw to a corner of the yard.

*

Because out of their subterranean suburbs
the ground squirrels are easy prey,
hawk buzzed and coyote snuffed.
Because I commune with the imbecile vultures,

it's all too easy to say a phantom kisses me.

They call me into frenzied frequencies
between a drive-by and a pledge drive:
The hull's torn open, we all go down.
When the news is over, it's over with.

The voice of wishful thinking,
a wet-mouthed nymph, rises in stereo.
Abandoned to differences of air,
I do the dead-man on the waves.

If I had the choice, I would take it.
Take the sky. Take the sea.
What would I have? Lovers pressing body
to body? Not exactly not at all.

Take the boat on the horizon.
It's tacking in, it's sailing away.
It being the most immediate antecedent
of the deceased, dear loved one I will not

name — at least, not in this lifetime.
At least, not at this moment
when the radio's off, and I'm tuning in
to the white noise of a lacerated sea.

Witness the waves against the rocks.
They will not turn the volume down.
Who is dying? What city burns?
Only the sea, which doesn't say, can say.

monologue for a father

Never is the way things used to be.
The life I used to live before.
A small king in a small town
& mountains . . .

silvered in cinematic black & white.

Night is *Out of the Past* starring
more of myself than I care to remember
& a soft discoursing woman,
poppies in the gold of harvest, high

on the tide of good luck &   GASOLINE—
a small world under the big sign
built like gallows.   [Bird shriek]

                Nightbirds assemble
private darkness, in my daughters' sky.
The Cordelia lie.

[Sings] *Too ra loo ra lie, my kingdom for a lullaby.*

                Never is between:
my retinue of *dark backward abysm of time*
& a filling station filled with limelight,

between my past and a smooth talker,
stranger in a black overcoat knowing:
Behind every man there's a femme fatale.
There's a double-cross & a cross undone.

This gangster night is noir, is silver,
is straight whiskey plus a .45, which equals
a slick-lipped dame at the roulette wheel,
or a cigarette punctuating darkness.

Or: night is *lady in white walking in with the moon,*
night is the never of never enough, as in
Baby, I don't care

& a full-screen kiss in milky light.
It's a net that catches the scandalized eyes
of voyeurs like flies, in theater-dark—

& more of myself than I could make up.

In this nightly version, I live
to climb around in my own skull,
contemplating my once Empire of Adoration.

Am I speaking now to an empty house?

Daughters of my blood, who do not love me?

Daughters with their Medusa hair.
Wanton. Bedaubed in rouge.
Turning dials on the Hi Fi—
music the house can't hold—

mocking the pounding of my Technicolor heart.
Abandoning me to bygone days of dogwoods

& the bedlamite expression of the moon . . .

& and these bird-fears.

I, who was king of swelling violins,
& a hash slinger named . . . Mabel? Delia?

 [Sings] *My kingdom for an alibi, too ra loo ra lie.*

I, rummaging dustbins of past lives.
Nightlives of martinis & snazzy hats
now blurred . . .

ELEGY FOR THE PRESENT MOMENT

The stepping stone never leaves its footprint.
The stone begat by stone, stone
with its placard, Washington, to paraphrase,
passed here on his way somewhere else.

Where a tree came and went, the road forks.
The sun pulling out its last sword, speaks
color the way color does: *tongue in the eye.*
Warm as a puddle of blood over the town,

the light stains the faux colonial façades,
the umbrellas like bones collapsing.
It wine-lights the coats ducking into shops,
startling mannequins in their glass sepulchers.

The sun lopped off, lops off the shadow of me.
Darkness crawls into a field of itself.
Time was, I was a boy in this town.
Time was and I cannot get a word in edgewise.

Today is yesterday in buffalo time.
The end of another workday for the dragonfly
marauding the stagnant pond for iridescence.
Discard for the raccoons eating human garbage.

It's whistling time under these noctilucent clouds.

No footprints recede into the distance,
unless these last slivers of red light
are what remains of a stellar walking,
this whole body of water the print
of one tremendous foot.

*

I have lived through two forevers now:
a forever of cowering until you sobered.
A forever now of china-white foam,

a third and final forever where green
water smears into the blonde coast,
the dark skyline crawling up.

The jailed ocean eddies past.
It isn't Irish water. Unless
this sea is coal and thunder,

a thousand kettles untended,
a city letting loose a long-held breath . . .
wake of cabbage plowed under.

*

Slipping from the coast like a breath —
or clothes from a body —
that's how I thought it should be.

The jetty trembled in gray light.
Arms and legs retracted
into a dark mass. That father was

not you. Beneath clicking
oarlocks, your labored
breathing, your protruding eyes

pleading . . . just that morning you
chewed like a lion, a sphinx,
dictating chores for the day, for

my lifetime. I tried to be invisible —
a glass in water —
to your fisherman eyes.

*

The tide takes what nobody has a right to.

You can't say what kisses you there,
under starlings two-by-two clouding the sky.

I was running in the gray darkness.

Island hopping, they wing
the harbor, they railroad the horizon,
then bank into the paved and parceled shoreline.

A perch here, a perch there,
Verazzano's Arcadia, "land of cool springs,
soft meadows and groves," slaked like a runway.

*Crickets were sawing in the grass, pacing me
with a small traveling island of silence.*

Grain by grain, the coast shuffles off.

*

Fishermen pull up what they did not
trawl for or grope, fully clothed,

                   in pressured darkness for:

3 sea robins, 3 rock crabs, 1 undersized flounder.

In the channel, tender leviathan, sand fills
your shoes, your ears . . .

The tide takes a kingdom of mostly water.

The real world's down here.
In the real world of my apartment,
the phone rings its underwater ring.
The sky files down a corridor of water.
Days eddy in and out of days.

Trees float, houses tumble past.
What sinks swirls in a current
of gravity gone haywire.
The wolf and the lamb and the one
missing shoe on equal foot.

Sinking is one way, a good way:
Eels in silky mud make good bedmates.
There's more inside the water than every thing:
handful of salt, pocketful of water.
Nothing I could nail into something larger.

A boy dismantling his toys
dreams of one gigantic machine.
Here, on the inside, I have one
over on him. Though I am
under and over and dead on.

Unbeknownst to the boy smelling
the pink of the backyard flowers.
Unbeknownst to the airplane circling
like a man looking for his house keys,
my neighbor's dog swallows its bark.

Trees walk, the general trees of my understanding;

treed in a waterwall of days.

II

Voices inside the ark:
Only
the mouths
were saved. Hear us,
o sinking things.
— Paul Celan, "Voices scored into"
    (tr. Heather McHugh and Nikolai Popov)

These milky breath-clouds
drift away like the old country,
defy gravity a moment,
join bodies of water,
unlit rooms of waves . . .

I am by nature
an odor of you, an air of you,
something less than I was before.
Harbor that you are. Ocean.
Island in the ocean.

Your breaking is the breaking of water:
father after father now a single undertow.
I walk among what you do not have
time for. *Spartina patens*, sharp
inedible grass that holds the world

to the world. Georgie Rogan,
carry your pail in your potato fist
across the straw-strewn farmyard.
I'll walk away whistling.
The tune, yours, a white lion, a lamb.

Big talker, crab shell in the wind,
I would be as you were
if I could go backwards.
What if it's true?
There's the wrong way and there's yours.

Three corners of the sail,
only one to fold in first.
A little cloud that shrouds me.
I live down here
on the corner of the mouth

and the ocean. I return
to this intersection, warm the air
that will not love me,
this water and light, fingers
that will not come to my mouth.

WEST OF HERE, NORTH OF TRUE

1

My lover, the new world,
winks like a city of gold.

Her belly is my meadow,
my swinging door. In her eyes

I am two silver dollars
and time on her hands.

I am the IOU spelled out
on her back. The one she holds

her breath for, kisses
the dust for. Flies do her

talking but it doesn't concern me.

I am just another meal.

2

No water to want, I drink
myself under, silver spurred,

sporting my ten-gallon hat,
my ten gallons of empty.

My horse is tethered in the wrong city.

My horse in a kingdom of mostly water.

Cowboys, drunk and dry, flop
in streets of airborne dust.

My horse tethered in the wrong city,
I hoof it out to the highway.

It travels into a world of small things.

It travels beyond the squinting of my eyes.

3

City of lips,

west of here, north
of her true lips, a line so soft,

so carefree I'd say it wasn't

all there. A dream of skin
on skin, I would not call any thing.

The stones without lips say
"sleep with me," but I'm with the skyline.

Stumbling dust devil in the streets
of her hands, the palaces of her eyes,

I, who have no name

to call her, call her bride for now.

The world once was solid,
rivers and bays so fish-thick
the Indians (legend goes) walked on water.
Flying at 35,000 feet, even the ground

is conjecture: love, your feet swell
in a simulacrum of ripening. They loom
large next to my book about John Smith
and his dream of America, his fish gospel.

Turning back a page,
everything happened, nothing's true.
If I told you that down there
a musket is being fired at a redskin,

that he takes off with a wave of plovers,
would that keep the plane from going down?
Between Paradise and *tabula rasa*,
the ax falls —

Cockles and mussels alive, alive . . .
If I told you Cibola and El Dorado were gilded
inventions next to mounds of fish, stinking,
would John Smith be as real as you?

And yesterday . . .
through the kitchen window,
the garden frozen in glass, tomatoes heaped,
tomatoes rotting on the vines, the red globe

ruptured when you put it in my mouth.

I want to hear what you hear, scattered
in voices you call by my name,
unassembled in throats of the air. Gulls

buckle in a gust. Sirens find the ear
in a parking lot, dissipate into the Sound . . .
The light on the water,

a wavering city held by invisible lines.

A blur of green, our first summer
shifted in the window.

Clams pissed their translucent architectures —
sun-wrenched into the air . . .
The green wall of trees kaleidoscopes

into the Sound even now, gazing into my eyes.
June, I remember, inhaled into the channel . . .

Marian, do you hear me
through the hole in the sky
where the roof was? The sky pouring in
with its ghost-weight, with its possibility
of traveling these distances . . .

Marian, what gleams in the frontiers —
in the running sand sometimes —
insisting in your sleep — in the flashing waves —
what streets maze into the currents . . .
the universal cannibalism of the sea.

The light trembles and rocks.

The Lord writes his pleasure,
then smears it away . . .

Sometimes, Lord, it's like water
spiriting through blue into cirrus clouds.
In the end, there's no end in sight.
Just as well: something wants
to build a nest in our skulls.
Cicadas never stop sawing in the trees.
The trees never fall down.

With this black robe, I espouse
to these people you who take no bride.
With this mirror, this cross, knife,
I lure a native with shiny things. Bloody
spouse in spirit, her eyes dim over scripture.
Wholly without names, the black marks
swarm like bees she is deaf to.

What is it that wants to carry away
this head on a stick? This head
looking down the path it came from?
A billion cornflowers line the way, flower-sky
where once upon a time the invisible hand
slapped and slapped. What you can't see
starts the wild grasses trembling.

ONE

My mutineer, I pitied you, taught you each hour . . .
More fish than man, more goat,

all bleat & blurb, bent gabbing to birds,
God had no time for you. I clothed you.

Made all purposes known to you:
Why woods, raked with sun-tined clouds

& ichorous colors of six o'clock in May . . .
Why trees, unearthed most chirurgeonly.

Now, with the pomp of a king's circuit,
you dream dreams of my fire-powders.

I see you in the flayed light of the sun.
I see *boy pushing wheel with stick.*

I have plantation of this isle —
I have the water's sorcery

with protestant pools, sun coveting water.
Even trees put on my misty airs:

Heretical trees that work themselves free,
industrious trees that lie down & make walls.

TWO

My flesh wears wisteria for want of clothes.
It's worn by the wind's breath —

a cold air that starts a thousand
instruments twanging, each an isle

of thunder & mother's voice fading.
My island is more islands — of green

& green & lightning bolt weather.

(I set the table, but no one comes)

It's the rain that chatters to phantoms,
speaks the tongue of a short-circuited brain.

It's the wind that comes down to bite me.
Inchmeal takes the rouge from the trees.

I am not afraid.
The matter at hand is out of hand.

Under branches cloaked with cloying fog,
I talk to birds & who can say who strips

away my skins & seaweeds, who kisses?

What nature abhors
is mostly itself. This canoe is mostly
nothing on this green wound, its ribs bared
like a hostage, decaying into the pond.
The hard and simple fact goes soft.

It would make a pretty picture.
It would make a pretty anything — but it isn't.
Under an arch of black birch branches,
it takes the shape of an unshapely mass
mired in what was once — the way

Hiawatha never was. The way
Longfellow and a dozen painters paddled him
into a sunset, the dream of Europe's America,
a distance of illuminated white birch
spires — sublime — rising above

what is
next to nothing, next to
the shores of Gichy Goomy. Don't cry,
Minnehaha, your lover won't hear
the cool-dark muck sucking

like no death song. Canoe,
where the meadow blossoms,
canoe, where saplings dig and stroke
the slow river of earth, queen,
more or less, of the August rain.

I went away, and you were a stone bell
struck, silently ringing . . .

Our red house, imperious at the end
of our street, winnowed away.

Bits of color drifted off.
The in-between spaces more main
                                in the end,

a swarm of hesitation, a beginning.

You were too heavy
                        for the bore of the matter.

Your brothers left the nets ungathered.
Your sisters left the babies to cry.
They stood, a mass of interlocked arms.

Incorpsed as it were, as if it were
                                possible to grieve.

The sun struck the door, and it was a knock.
The wind kicked-in from the harbor,
                                and it was true . . .

The maimed rites of seasons rescheduled their events.

The long winter reigned all year.
Spring brought its own wet winter.
Summer its desolate brown winter.
And fall . . .

So much goes without saying.

You were saying the blue bicycle, the sailboat,
and the flower all ride in the same night.

The city is over here.

You were saying, *in my small town*
the broken conches are the biggest words around.

You with your newspaper and coffee.
You gawked into the harbor's mouth.
It was clear no boat would come

through the narrow channel the coldest night
of the year, but you waited and you said it,

this talk piles up at the feet of your departure.

Wake-up, wake-up,

the city is over here —

I wait for a shot in the back,
the earth being so round and empty
and all, but not at all small.
The gun's only son is my reckoning.

I have a nail and no shoes.
I have shoes and no horse.
I have a 20-acre kingdom
and no neighbors to ogle at it.

Twenty miles from any neighbor —
or three days by horse for the man
with no horse. A skeleton away,
my neighbor holds court with flies.

When I say, "look who's talking,"
the river goes dry and quiet.
I think about prairie grass,
which is the gun waiting to happen.

When the clouds barge in with bullets,
I dance their rain dance and sing.
Then I notch the stick, same as always.
My buckboard tied to its post,

I wait for the holes in my horse to heal.
All night long the rain pokes
through the roof, through the trees.
It shoots off at the mouth, like laughter.

NATURAL HISTORY

Everything that is right or natural pleads for separation.
— Thomas Paine

Packets of light, glances without faces,
dart between leaves where we gather
the horse bones somebody left behind.

A dust of nothing in particular kicks up.

It swirls in the angled light
in this life-size diorama, billows
around our feet like translucent blood.

The dust happens a thousand times,
clouds our eyes till we're blind with seeing
nobody. It's a surface we walk into,

a statement we inspect the ground for.
Tooth and jawbone. The dead bleached
of all desire. In the aftermath,

a dog barks in the subdivision, a train
howls. Space rearranges, trees leave
out the ocean, its wrinkling and peeling

(the first settlers could see it from here).
Skunks watch. Poison slithers
behind the cloak of trees (smiling, we think).

The wind rushing in our dry ears
is nobody walking westward still,

dust of nothing in particular kicking up.

Half-hearted aqueduct, river of eyes streaming

Pavement and what travels over

What stands erect, dream of trees, of evaporation

Our Lady of Anonymous Face in a Crowd

All circles, the mouths of a river opening

Gulping light and air I would see by, breathe by

Our Lady of Nobody Holds Me

Blue fingernails and undinal white she leases

Shark to blood, boy to the implausible

The girl on the bus walks down the aisle, descends

Disappears into the crowd, the whole bus sighing

Such dry fantasy, a multiplication of faces

Schooling down corridors I can't remember

I remember — blur of green blouse, of jet black hair

Darling phosphorous, darkling eyes of fish

I have always wanted citizenship in your city

These fish-thoughts of you in a satisfactory sea

Our Lady of Towers, Lady of the Angel-Void

III

With a mercy that outrides
The all of the water, an ark
For the listener; for the lingerer with a love glides
Lower than death and the dark;
A vein for the visiting of the past-prayer, pent in prison.

— Gerard Manley Hopkins,
  "The Wreck of the Deutschland"

Inheritance

What's this I leave for him?
A house with more rooms than the sea.
At an edge like Fra Angelico's blue, stones
lifted me, the water receded, fish cried.
Did he hear it? Did he fling himself
like a withered wave? No, he minced
a sand taste with his teeth and spit out
the ghost grains. In the transparent sky,
he sees nothing, says, perhaps, "he was . . ."
What *does* he remember? My two hands
floating away like oak boards he would
nail into something useful. A shelf
for shells, a ship to find holes in
and mend until the next leak springs.
He won't look up from his canned soup.
Talk doesn't get things done, so he
must be talking, stealthful and stealing,
saying what I would say if I had a say.

Sugaring-Off Time

In the Currier & Ives of my mind,
it's sugaring-off time, the weather tastes of you.
I remember maples caving in Park Street.

The house going up, the house coming down.
Red square of it smeared across my eyes.

O in the black of my head.

White neck pouring out against gravity.
Sea of black shoulder. Black eyes undressing.

O, I say and turn to what's left unsaid.

My eyes with the swallows construct
biographies in the eaves, daylight
distilling in amber, honeyed essence of . . .

I want to say the moment's *soul*,
time-being liquefied & oozing between boards.

Flies stumble, clear of conscience.

Light, my pilgrim, you're not the one
I'm looking for. Shadow, my pilgrim,

I follow you till you follow me around.

The House Changing Hands

Our street no longer stumbles
into trees. The sign is gone
along with the dead end.

British-green BMWs lead each other
by invisible threads past houses
in colors of nouveau New England's

mauve and robin-egg blue.
A professional couple in a swath
of Kentucky-blue-green grass

ply their beautiful, shiny-faced daughter
on her first bicycle where my brothers
scraped the bottoms of their rowboats

and spread their nets to dry.
My father, the carpenter, built the house.
He no longer fixes the windows I break.

My father, the pilgrim, left nothing behind.
My mother left *Little House on the Prairie.*
Sometime yesterday I walked 5 miles to school.

This Is Here, It Is Now

Always the glittering mineral mountain
of the horizontal, the quarter moon
of shoreline, the rockweed's iodine odor.

How many times have I walked into a dot?
Turned back empty handed?
Come home in the hands of something big?

These father hands are my hands,
sharpening a saw, rasping and traveling

(my eyes are plunging into the work).

Here, I am the widowed mother pouring coffee
for the son back from war in a piece,
and I am a piece of the son who remembers

the father in another lifetime crying,
"Madre de Dios!" on an Argentine train,
shooting trees, shooting empty forest.

Here, I return like Vespucci, sailing
downhill from the Mountain of Purgatory.

Here, an egret would launch into a shell of sky.

Museum

Something's in the smell of their coats
—without them—suspended at the back
of the schoolhouse. Something's in
the hooks without coats. The bell unrung.

I mop up clods of dirt where the farmboys
loosened it from their shoes with sticks.
I mop what isn't dirty,
sweeten with pine and water.
The pine odor is stronger than a pine's.

The trees hold the blacksmith hostage,
release him slowly through their leaves.

In the doorway of the reconstructed barn,
no haymakers dance. They are framed
up the hill in the Art Building. My broom

is a pathetic dancer who has no supervisor.
It snags splinters, leaving its little limbs.

The curator, who calls me son,
explains the past is what you make it.
I am a good worker until he exits the service gate.

To the Revenant

I think you are sinking in, wind-pockets
fingering the surface, and in the lull,
the fabric tightens over your half-dead body.

blue   losing   code blue   nothing   breathing

And if I look over my shoulder at you,
if I follow . . .

you were still standing at the sink, the broken cup
in hand, a shouldered silhouette against the window,

you would not look at me, would not speak,
muted there in the backlight,

the one that blurred into the blue
of the car was someone you wouldn't,
couldn't call back . . .

23 24 30 37   a pulse   coming   steady   coming

A blade of air in the lung tissue,
a million tongues, the skin, licks up the cold-damp.

An accident of light collides around your face,
joyous pool, I would follow, given that choice.

The Promise

          . . . not unlike the red hue
of the air just before supper, the light sheathed
the serrated leaves and the unhinged screen door.

Returning to the gated ways,
to the Dorset farm where we played tea,
hereto I come to view a voiceless ghost.

Touching the white of your dress
as you read, unseen constellations reigned,
and I longed after another's lost love:

old Thomas Hardy finds again
an ichthyosaur vertebrae broken free
of the sea bottom, a warm eye I want

to live in because it might let me, because
I want to pick-up its accent.

If the trees arch any more, I will fall.

The red brick factory demands a gaze,
corners blurring, leaves bleeding in the river.

Even these residuals of light feel like a presence.

The Smell of Forever

They broke my brother's nose again,
the one my father — all hands —
fashioned after a fashion

on a Hercules figurehead,
shipless on the green, banking
on harbor mud. My brother,

the vessel, stood like a shadow
smelling forever in the dead-fish air.
I find it restored — broken, less

aquiline (some vandal trying to undo
history or get it right). Father

could not hold the invisible ship together.

Circa 1870 — the ship sinks,
sends a wake in these waters.

Circa 1969 — the mutinous captain
watches the tide shipping out.

Circa 1986 — a little sail,
the broken nose casts a shadow.

All the Time in the World

Finally the unnumbered house
identified by the music's back beat—
it leaps from the darkness, withdraws.

Up the stairs, winding—
a crack of light wobbling between
the floor and a door, guides me

to the one voice in a party of voices.
Then there are faces, more many
than one. I drink a beer among the dancing.

*

In the rattle of bottles and cans
the homeless man descends our porch.
Sliced through the blinds, he lumbers

like Bigfoot breaking through branches
to some drunken hag—I think—
or an empty lean-to in the woods.

*

All the time in the world, all the time, and the ship

smashes down from the mantel. Nothing was not a symbol.

Everyone said the ship went down with the man.

IV

They said to him, "Tell us who you are that we may believe in you."

He said to them, "You examine the face of heaven and earth, but you have not come to know the one who is in your presence, and you do not know how to examine the present moment."

— The Gospel of Thomas

THE BLOUSE KEEPS OPENING

Chainsaw: insect burrowing into summer.

Air leaves things, the neighborhood exhales.

Signs read "Cathedral Pines,"

as if vision could be installed into trees,
trees grow more treelike.

As if a forest would pine into houses,
the sky unbutton, all music and Mary.

Some things you *can* count on:
Sirens. Speed. Hovering faces.

The shrunken woman in the ambulance.

The world dovetails into her:
Mother of my days, the street beds down in fog.

The white accelerating from white flowers —
the pockets of air, pockets of a woman I'll never know.

Whatever it is that never comes keeps coming:
Cicadas. Fat sizzling. Watched water steaming.

For now: succession of days,
tomatoes renouncing ripeness,

tomatoes I would smother ripe in a paper bag.
For now, the yard is a blouse of green.

A buzzard lollygagging above the not yet dead,
rises into confusions of air.

It opens the yard with its flying,
enters a weather wholly its own:

The scavenger's red eye weather.

Just like that? The sky cracked,
she tumbled down, broken
like a songbird winged?
It's what the boys, the stretcher bearers,
never had time not to believe:

it couldn't be otherwise.
One boy looks over his shoulder,
to an absent father in a breeze.
At least I imagine a son
left to fight and fend for himself.

Here, cowbells are only wilted flowers.
Like God's hair in her hand, they slump
from ringing forms to lifeless mass.
Her bandaged eyes blind her to the decay
of the last good things she saves.

To remember: a verb reflexive in their tongue
— unknown to her until now. Fairy-tale figure
in a smoke-clogged world, the children,
the fire beaters proceed, feel the charge
of delivering a frail

baby sister. So much brown field, so much
gray air, no one would think of hope.

For her we must be macaques on a limb,
head pressed, for life, into wet matted head.

We live in this setting without name or address.

We don't leave the house for days.
We make the long walk to the car,

and the longer walk back in memory
                    to our house in the trees.

Our arms hang empty at our sides.
The new snow gives in to a patch of earth.

We peer into the dark spot, into that room,
                    like humans

switching off a light. We listen
to the stillness. Its breathing.

In that body of darkness,
in that closed-off room,

daddy's girl is immense in her sleep.
She must be beautiful by now.

Inconsolable sorrow, we cradle her

like humans, very much like humans.

Nothing's true when the sea's wrong. Not my hands on the
body. Not the body in ashes spread thin and white and
loose again. The sea is dead wrong, the sea with ashes in
its mouth thinks it's a rose garden. Birds bird past the
disobedient flowers, being cardinal and red. Every thing
birds away. Jaded sea, a billion years old, I cannot see a
garden in the surface. I look, as into a glass case—just
glass in those green eyes, quick and unfinished as thought.
Being slab of meat, being son of goggle-eyed fish, loose
flesh follows me: Spear. Sponge. Tide. Eyes disfigured in
dead water—water hands itself away to empty sky. Water
that was skin, assaulted from the inside, climbing from
bone. Taking the softness away. In the parable of
evaporation, the sleeper wakes from the meat world.
In this impossible version: a seagull: the whole sky
circling. *Ashes ashes* drifting into the Sound: soft facts
into a fictional sea.

AS ONE WITH FOOT IN MOUTH

As flesh unfleshed, as fleshment of.

As one with tomahawk in skull,
no longer headlugged,

as one used to think:
I can see you

when I die, I die
a little faster.

As stray air brushing bare boards.
As light bending over a pair of shoes,

as musty coat holding the sole remains
of human shape.

As flood, as *as* . . .
profusion of darkness, red and yellow dahlias,

a chest of drawers, all furniture confounded.
All gathering together.

As aimless gust, as indefatigable fingers.
As washing machine pounding in a room above.

All the room a heart
and this corner of the world

a corner of Appalachia.
As lackadaisical flies,

barefoot tikes, green and purple Popsicle-mouths
open for more than a green wave of trees

in a corner of a skull.
As alien size this space.

As snake-tongued branches tongue.

As St. Francis tells the birds.

LIKE FREEDOM

Song of a Chain Gang

In the blue night of a crime spree
I trade larceny for my legacy.
I get Sunglasses watching me seeing
myself in his mirrored eyes.
Myself beaten blue, myself undefeated.
In penitentiary — impenitent —
a little less than fearless —
prophesy to bones.   *A little less*

                        What's inside me —
a flame strutting past cigarette trees —
smolders in the humidity of cells.
A pin-up girl tears the breath from me,
the little-shit boy from the man I am.
Lord, smite us in our chains.

                        I escape. And I'm escaping
into a whitewashed wall of morning.
Myself a dark stain in that screen,
an instinct for river and stream.   *A lost scent*
Sunglasses can't hold me in flashing eyes.
Call it: illumination is to be bad by prayer.
Call it: veritable ark upon the shoulders.
A dinghy will do, a dinghy or a bed,
a bed of a thousand lies will do.
I'd lie like a prince. I'd search neglect —
a mountainous rush of blood —
a moonshine in the rocks and no distillery.
This is called: the life of a galaxy.

                        I was not called —
but this ain't finished 'til it's over.
Tell him I'm flying into an open field,
a red sunset walking away.
Tell him I am and I am   *flying*

OUTLAWS, ACCORDING TO THE MOVIES

They drive into a north synonymous with the way
out, as in the Unabomber, draft dodgers, oblivious

forest conversing with wind it doesn't understand.

Orchestral surges with an inclination to swerve
close to the cliff, drawing them over the next ridge.
One imagines floating down the river, face up.
The other repeats a phrase from the radio,
Stacks of unidentified . . .
lumber, boxes? Not *bodies.*

Streams of light, they would escape the river.
Being what they are, fleshly versions

of stars, they follow its winding
like a fact they cannot get straight.

*

Old Testament rain: exaggerated sloppiness.

The rain means *circumstances beyond our control.*
The rain means they really want to kiss.

On the third day they continue in amber light,
yoked to the road. Hours lost in the telling.

Kingfisher footage.
Hovering over the fact of them,

the Bonnie and Clyde of them.
An air of machine guns and prohibition

whiskey about them, they could be:

Rebels of Lost Causes.
Freedom Fighters after the Fact.

*

Kingfisher footage with voice-over:

The problem with the bodies is that they
are keys to how history will be told.

Do they see themselves in this river?
Its sure career through incorruptible mountains?

River of boys drowning in a one-time showing
someone somewhere views every day,
the long, brown chests running into sand.

River of mosquitoes patrolling the nationalized air,
mosquitoes finding the ear behind all that hair:
unacknowledged state insects of their minds.

The radio's river of reportage and a song
of private resistance, something about a car,

a stranger, river they're just beginning to enter.

IN THE EROGENOUS ZONE
OF THE BODY POLITIC

Everything up to now *was*.
Former Soviet Union. Eastern Block
cigarettes infesting clothes and hair.
Breeze carrying news of the slaughterhouse.

On the actual news tanks circled the TV tower.
Tanks fired into the Parliament
while I was wanting nothing more
than you, at once girl and lissome

and flowers on a Chagall postcard always
floating sideways in weightlessness.
A bed and a town hovered next to Christ
in the painting while around me birch, pine,
concrete block houses rose from razed landscape.

You were not there, and hardly was I.
I was more like a shadow sidling up
to you, shape meeting exactly your body's
long curve. The slender lightbulb of it,
in a room countryless as white sheets,

the mouth-darkness of a floor,
walls like arms tightening . . .

Now, I am judging and disposing of roses:

Is it kinder of memory to dwell on desire
or the Estonian flag of the horizon?
sky: blue   trees: black   earth: white

I pledge allegiance to the present moment:

The Bogart break out in *Dark Passage*
where everything depends upon
a beautiful painter and a car
motoring over the Golden Gate,
sleek and lipstick, its fins encouraging
the first democratic air.

NOTES

"Out of the Past"
   The title is from the film starring Robert Mitchum. The song lyrics in italics are from Emmylou Harris.

"Small Traveling Islands"
   The italicized material is taken from *The Sound and the Fury.*

"The Old Hunting Grounds"
   The title and setting of the poem are taken from a painting by Worthington Whittredge.

"New World Narratives"
   This poem takes language from Cotton Mather and John Smith, as well as *The Tempest.*

"The Wounded Angel"
   This poem is a response to Hugo Simberg's painting of the same title.

"As One with Foot in Mouth"
   The italicized material is taken from Emily Dickinson's letters.